M is for Mom

Celebrating the woman who nurtured, loved, and raised you.

KINGDOM PUBLISHING

Honor your father and your mother, that your days may be long in the land that the LORD your God is giving you.

Exodus 20:12 ESV

Copyright © 2019 by Tracy Fagan

Interior and Exterior Design: Tracy Fagan
Illustration by Vecteezy

All rights reserved. This book or any portion thereof may not be reproduced or used in any manner, digital or physical, whatsoever without the express written permission of the publisher except for the use of brief quotations in a book review.

Scripture quotation is from the ESV® Bible (The Holy Bible, English Standard Version®), copyright © 2001 by Crossway, a publishing ministry of Good News Publishers. Used by permission. All rights reserved.

Printed in the United States of America

ISBN-13: 978-1-7322879-8-3

Kingdom Publishing
PO Box 653
Parker, CO 80134
www.Kingdom-Publishing.com

For additional ideas for each letter, visit www.kingdom-publishing.com/m-is-for-mom

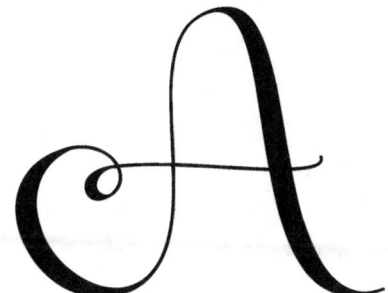

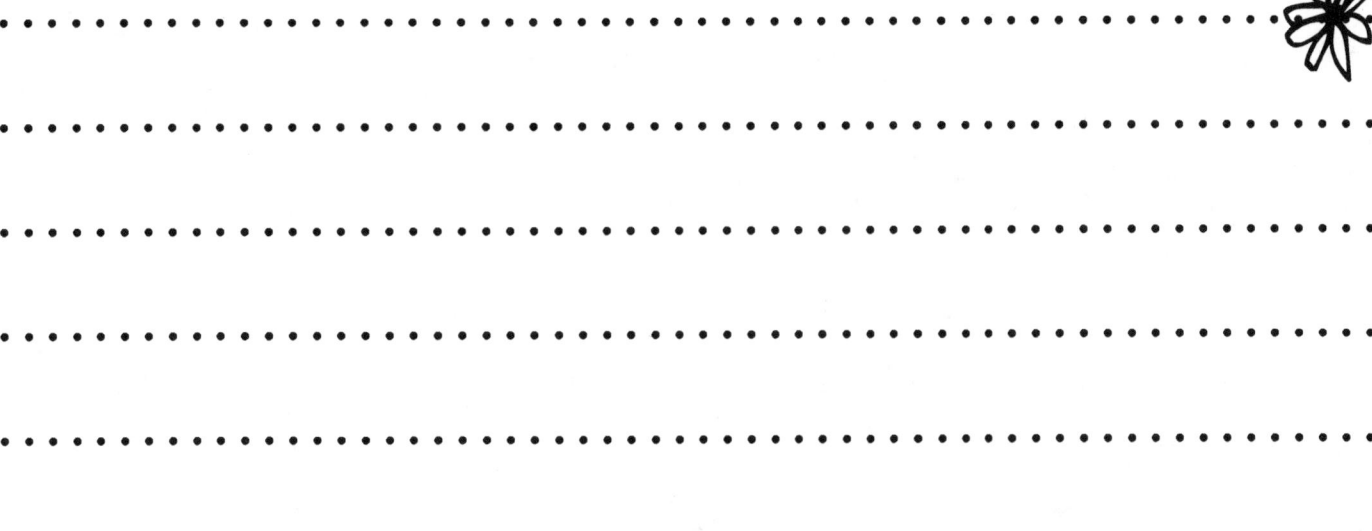

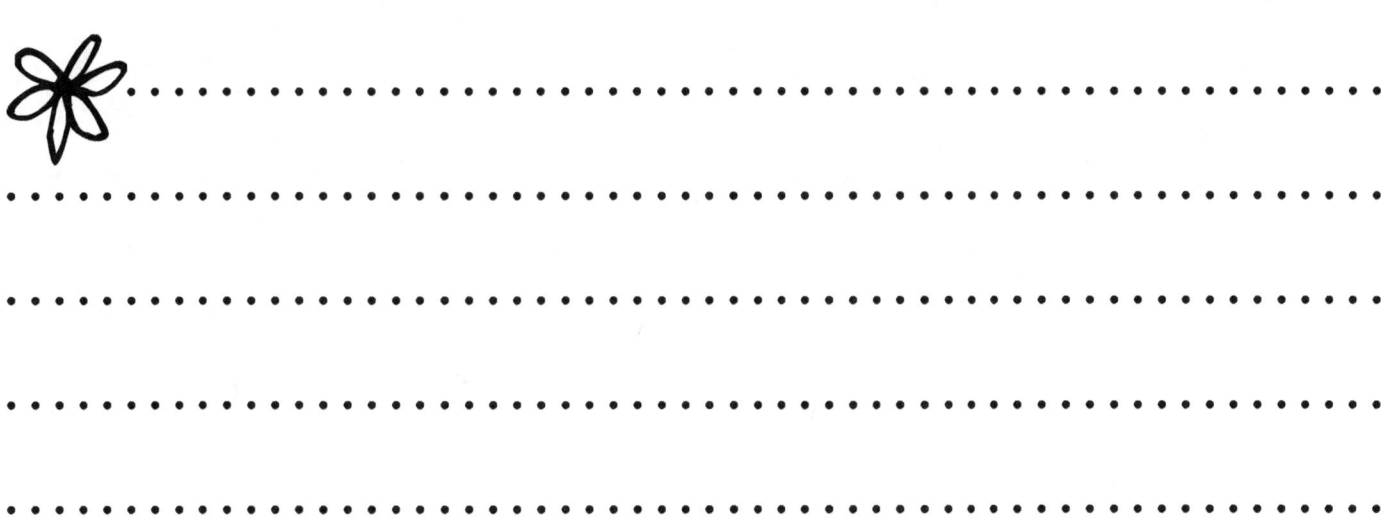

....
....
....
....
....
....

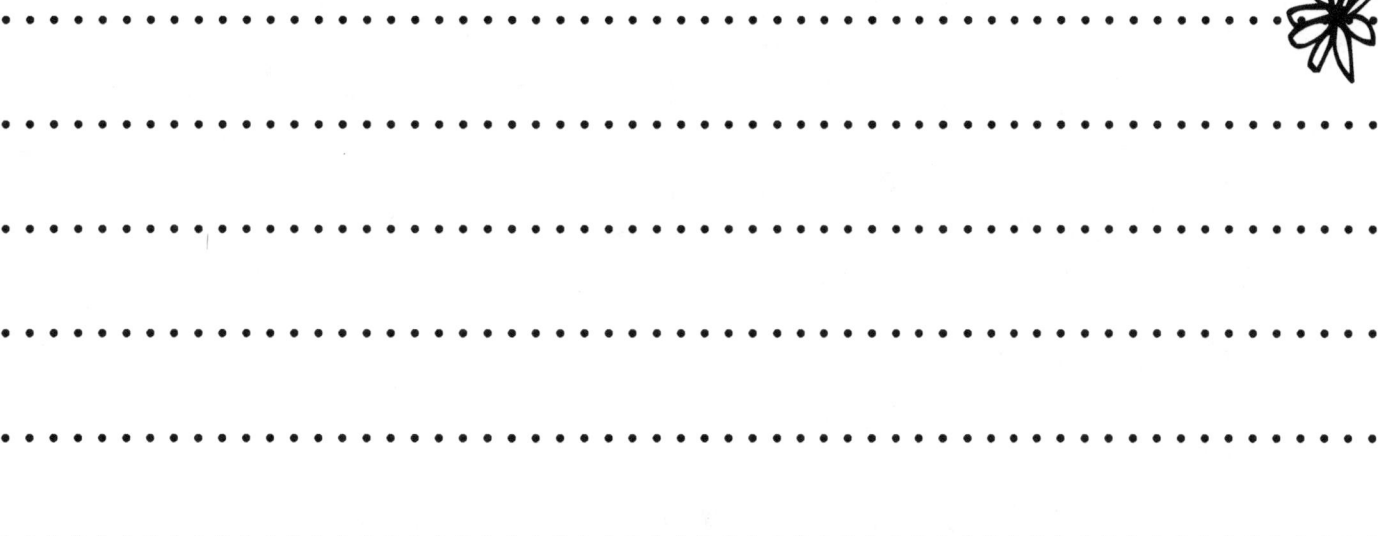

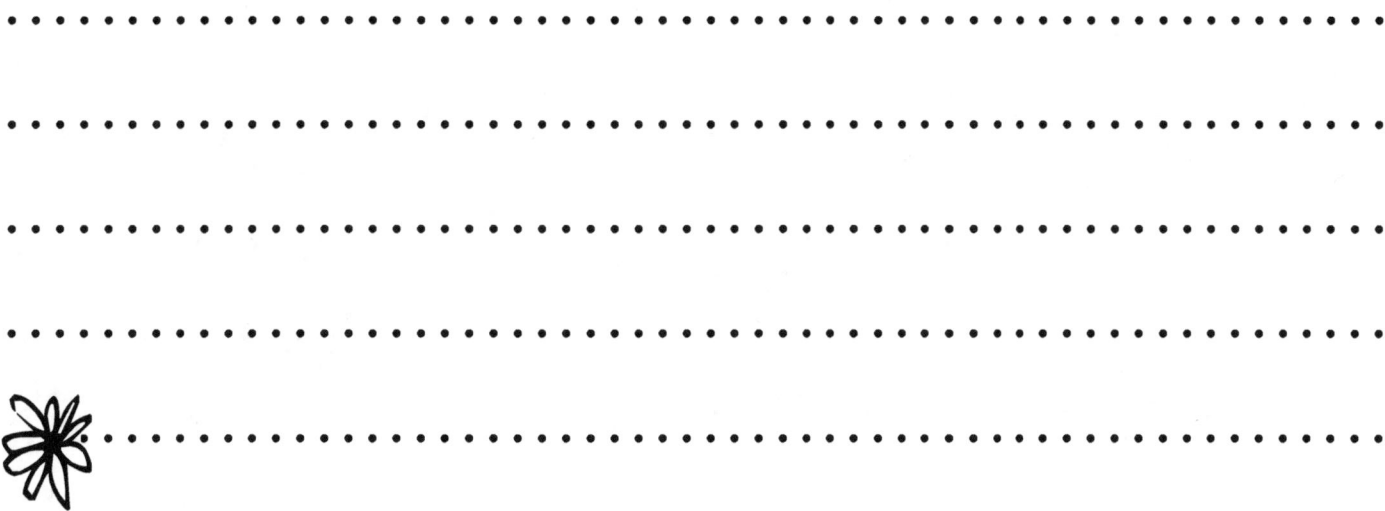

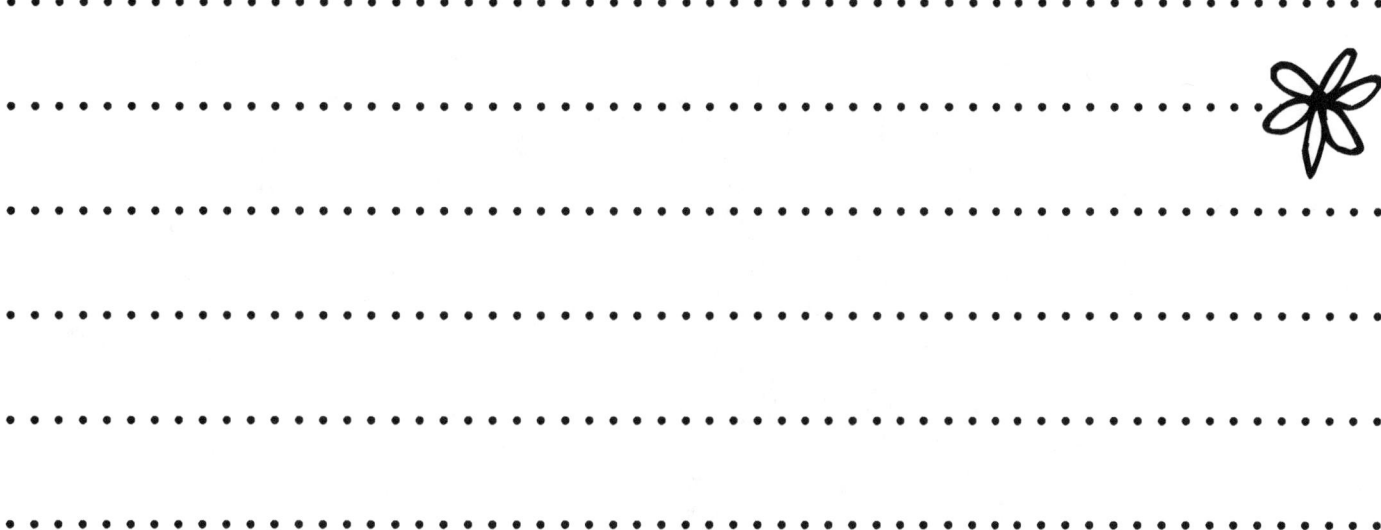

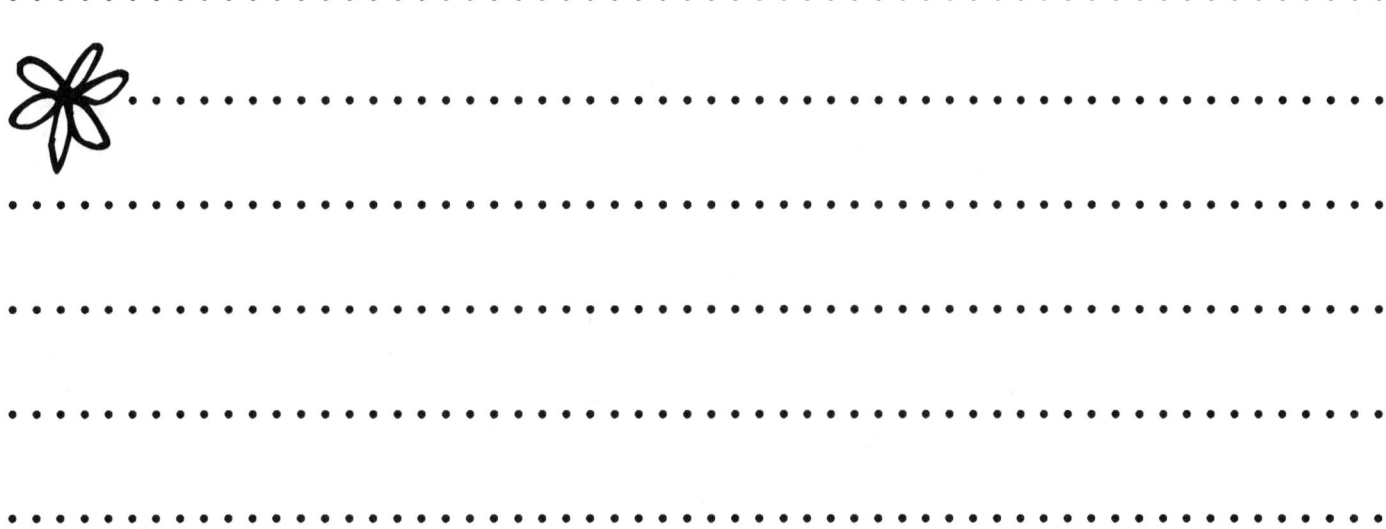

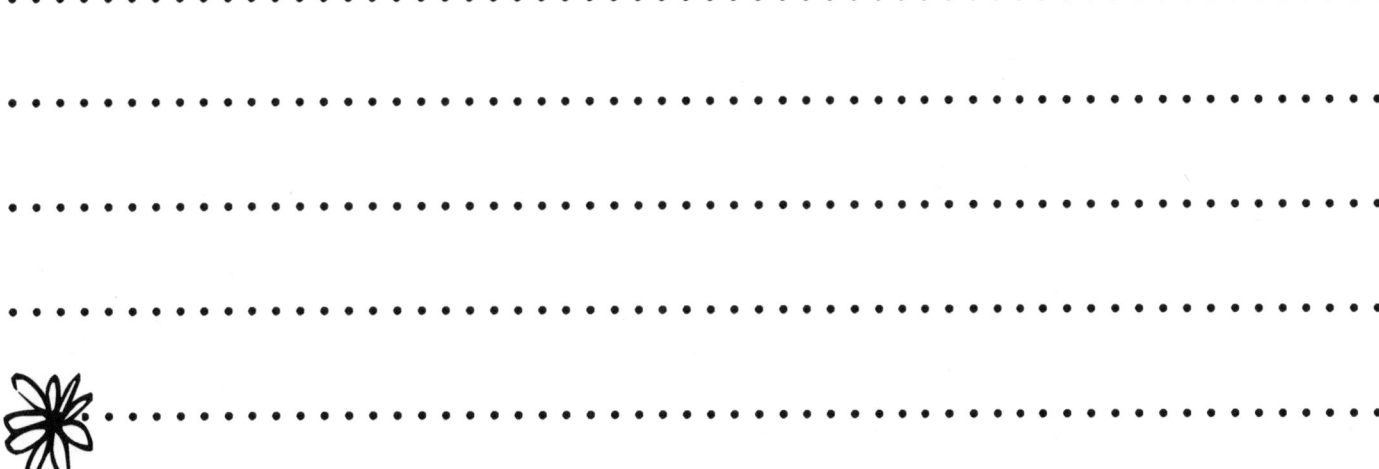

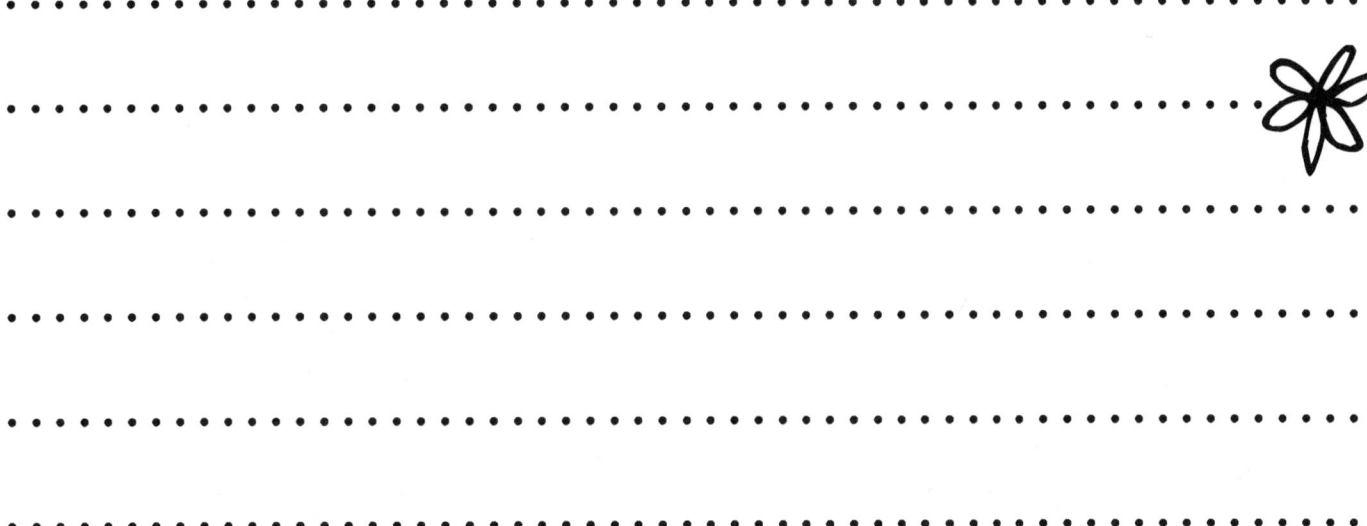

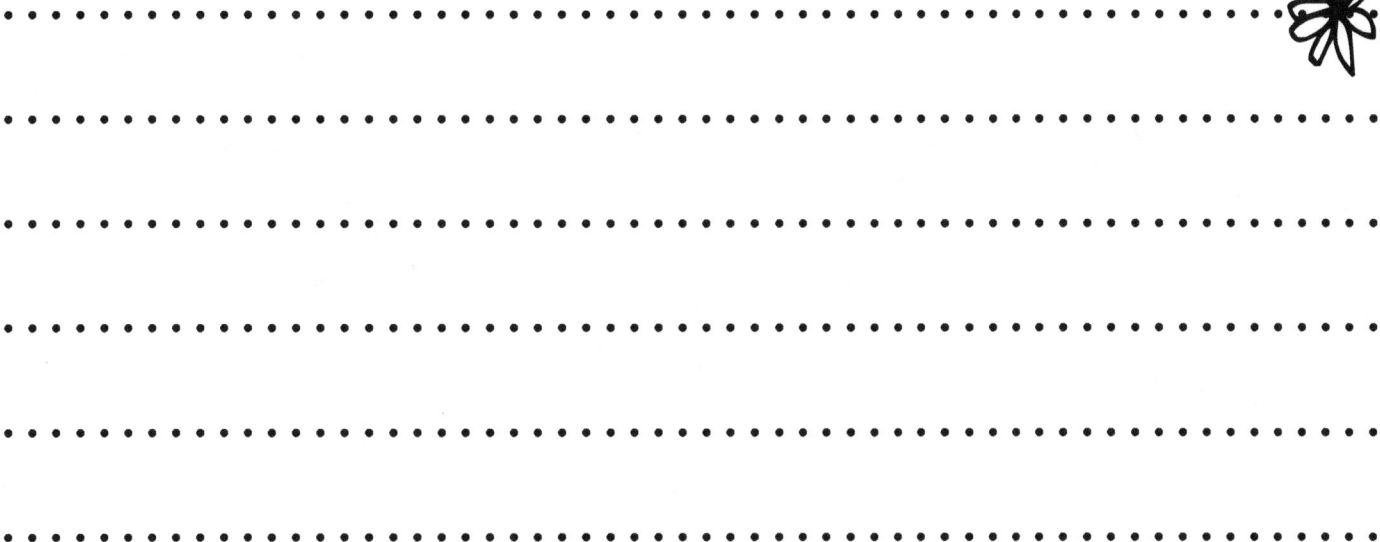

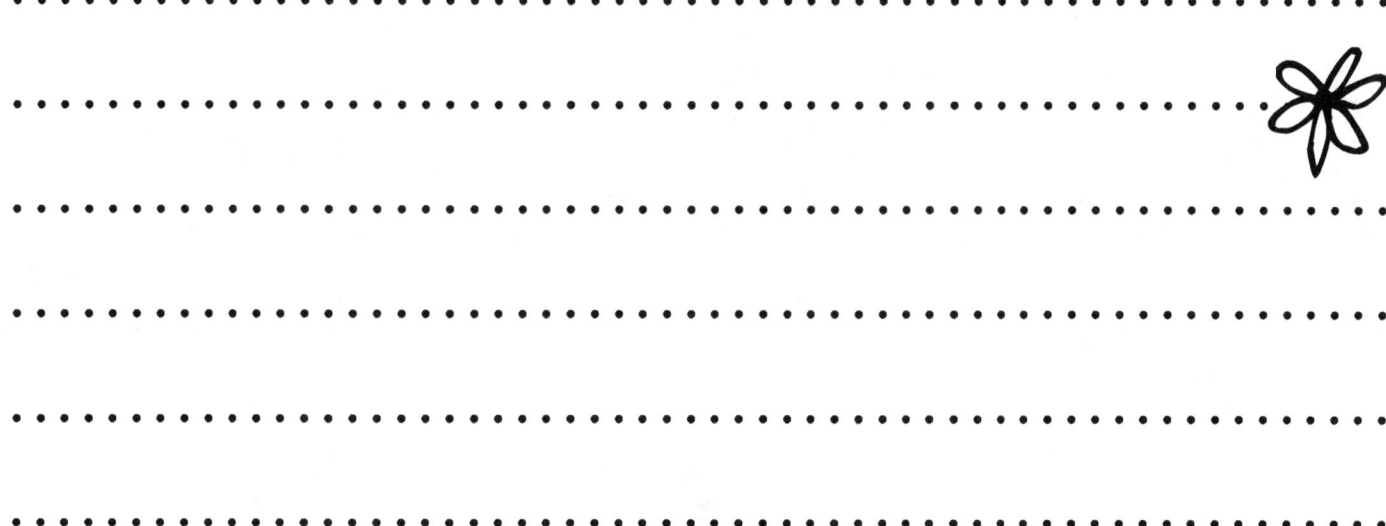

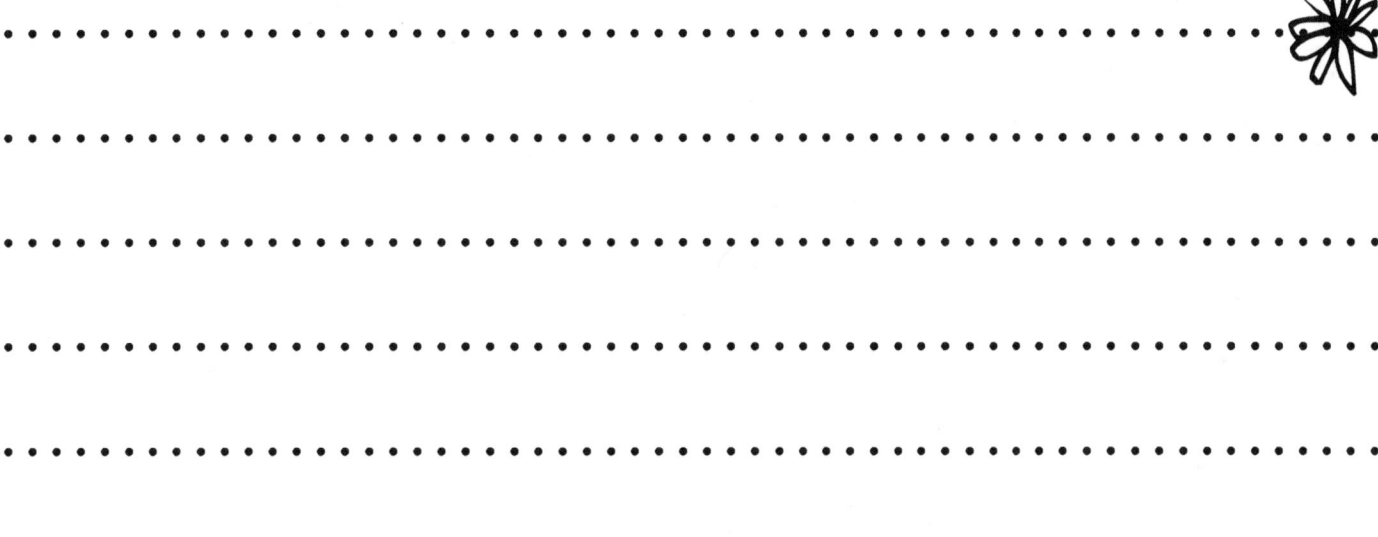

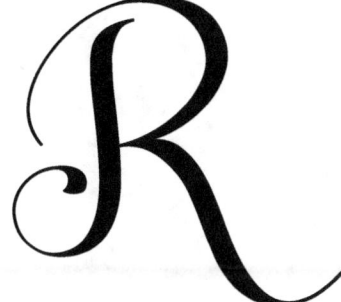

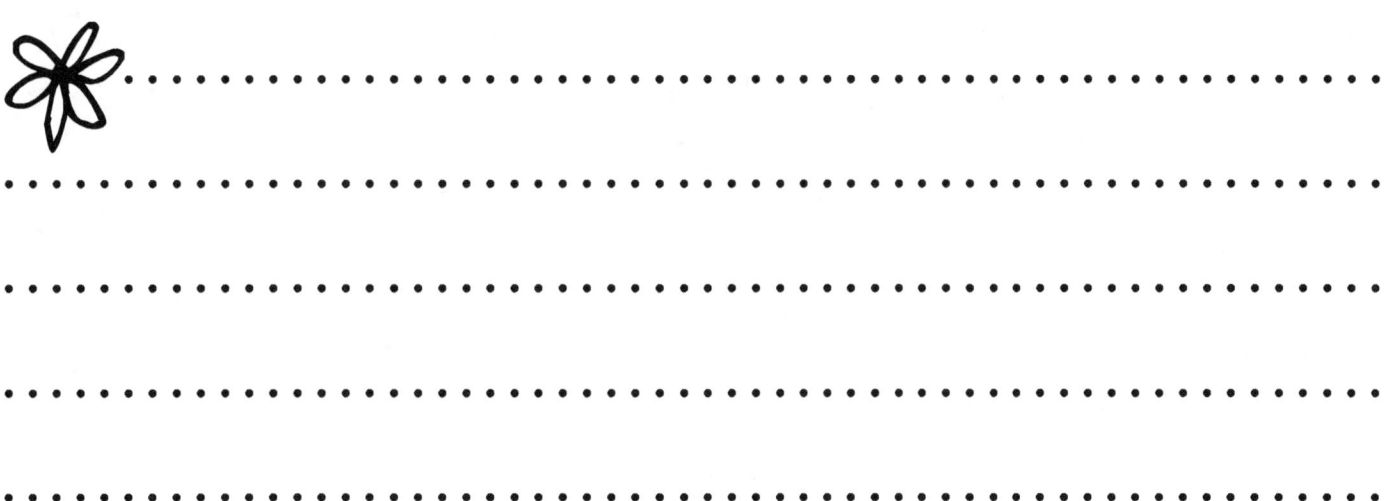

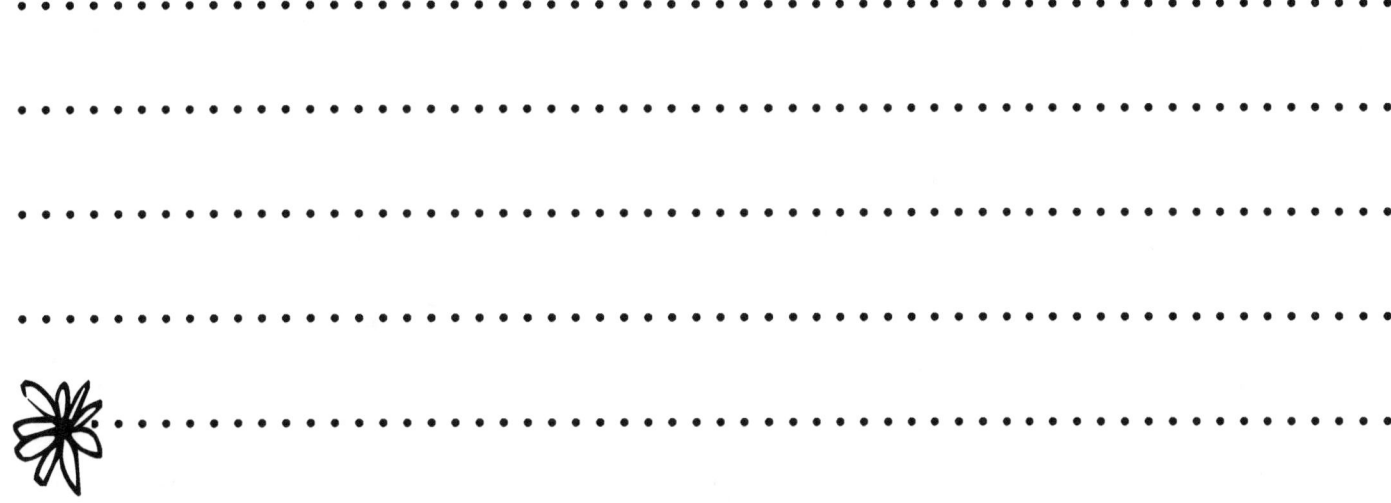

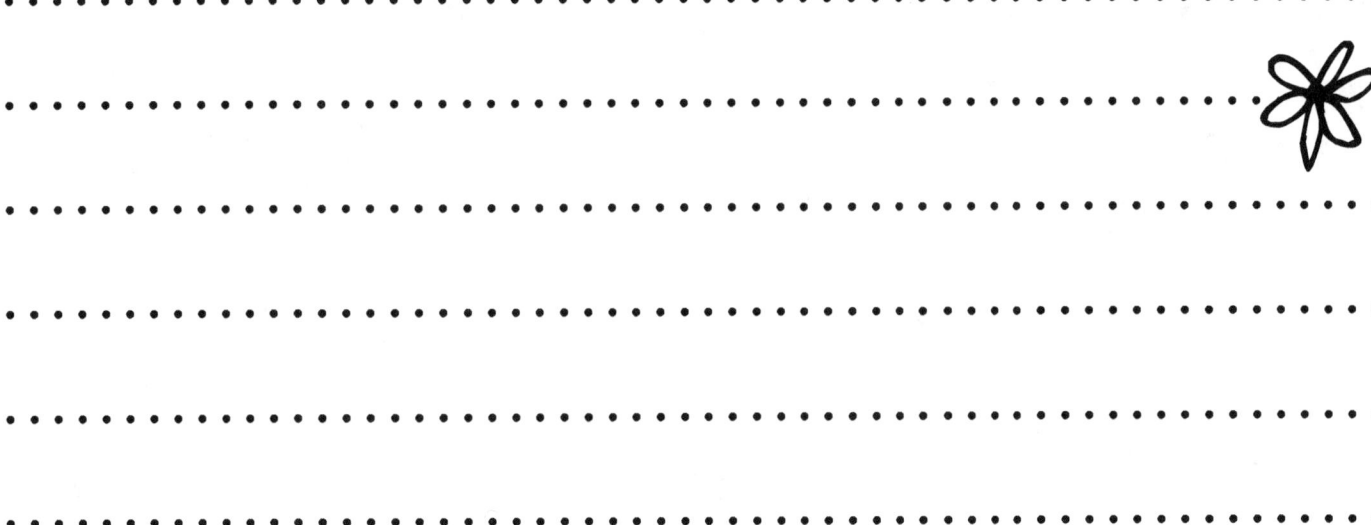

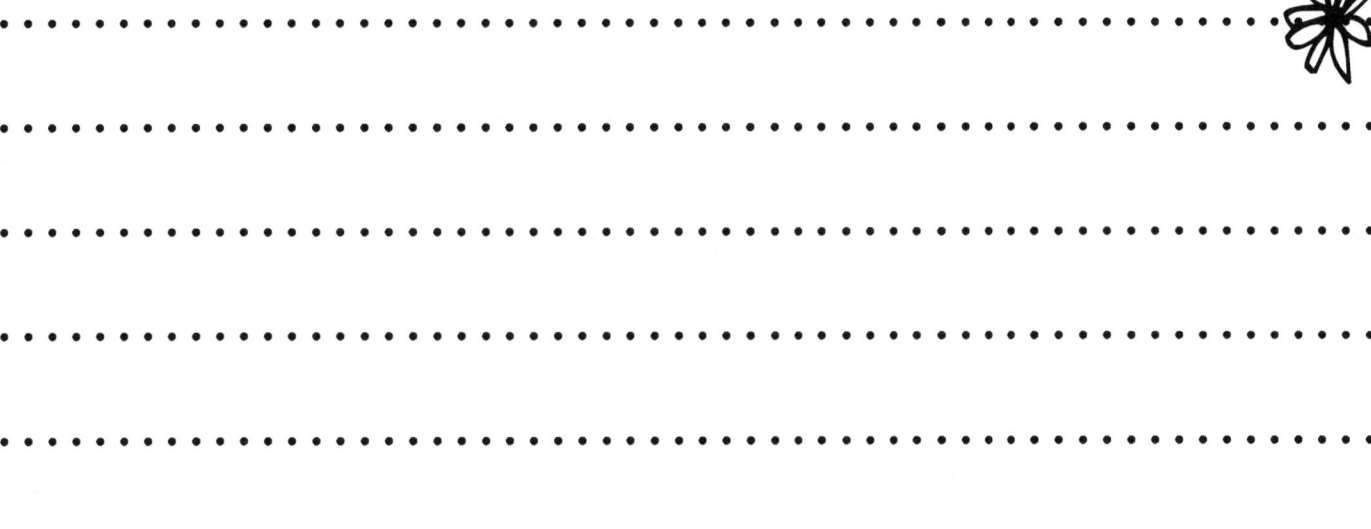

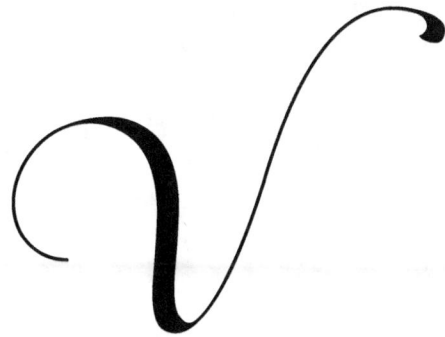

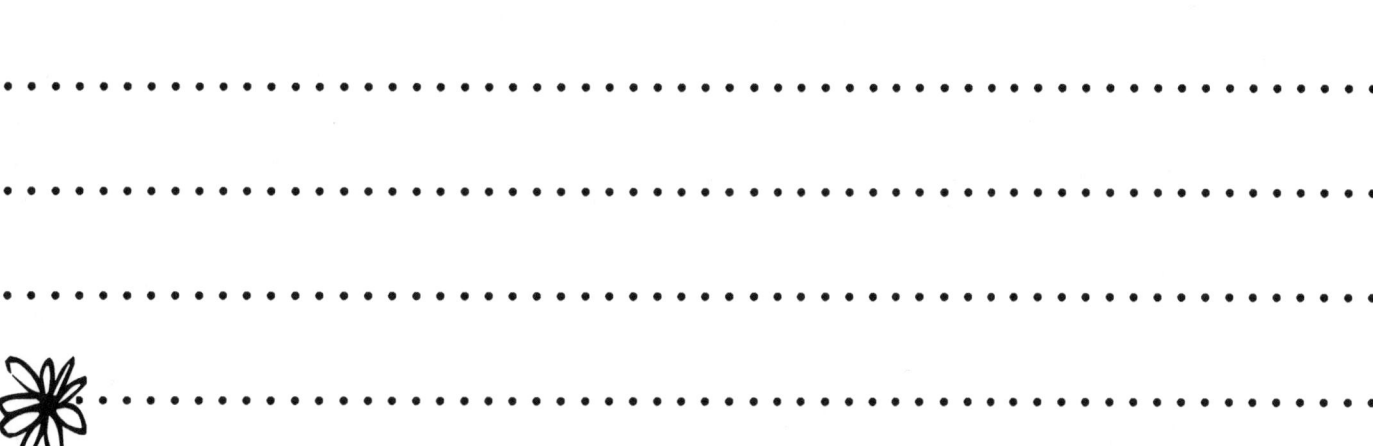

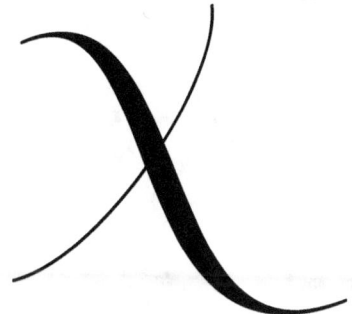

....
....
....
....
....
....

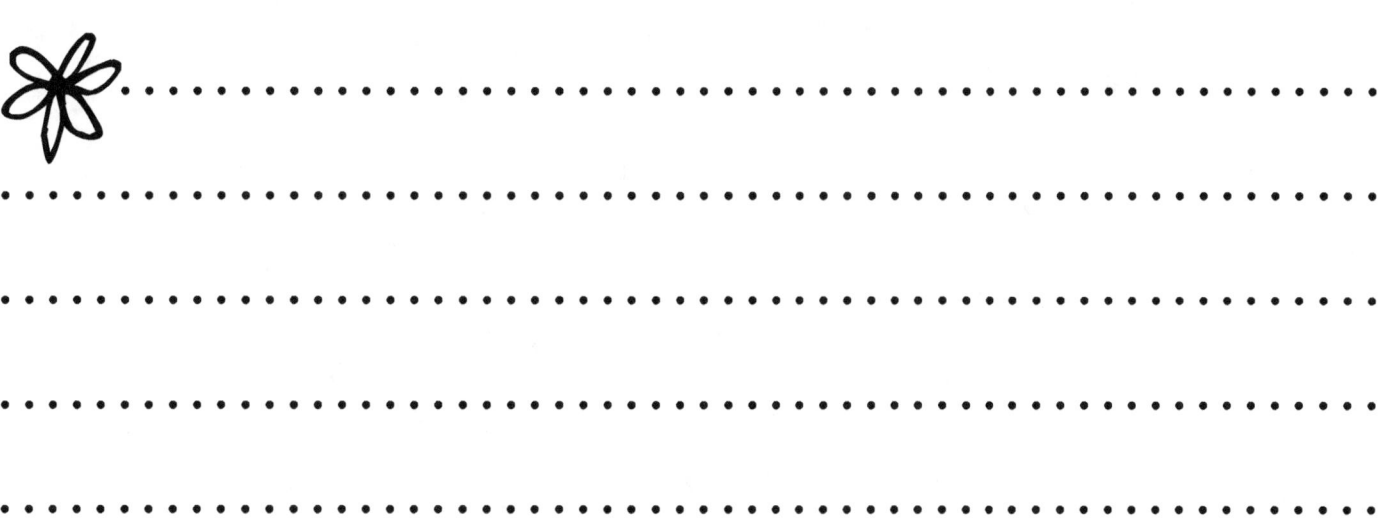

www.ingramcontent.com/pod-product-compliance
Lightning Source LLC
Chambersburg PA
CBHW051424070526
44584CB00023B/3567